1930—1939

Yearbooks in Science

1930—1939

NATHAN AASENG

Twenty-First Century Books
A Division of Henry Holt and Company
New York

Twenty-First Century Books
A Division of Henry Holt and Company, Inc.
115 West 18th Street
New York, NY 10011

Henry Holt® and colophon are trademarks of
Henry Holt and Company, Inc.
Publishers since 1866

Published in Canada by Fitzhenry & Whiteside Ltd.
195 Allstate Parkway, Markham, Ontario L3R 4T8

Library of Congress Cataloging-in-Publication Data
Yearbooks in science.
p. cm.
Includes indexes.
Contents: 1900–1919 / Tom McGowen — 1920–1929 / David E. Newton — 1930–1939 / Nathan Aaseng — 1940–1949 / Nathan Aaseng — 1950–1959 / Mona Kerby — 1960–1969 / Tom McGowen — 1970–1979 / Geraldine Marshall Gutfreund — 1980–1989 / Robert E. Dunbar — 1990 and beyond / Herma Silverstein.
ISBN 0–8050–3431–5 (v. 1)
1. Science—History—20th century—Juvenile literature. 2. Technology—History—20th century—Juvenile literature. 3. Inventions—History—20th century—Juvenile literature. 4. Scientists—20th century—Juvenile literature. 5. Engineers—20th century—Juvenile literature. [1. Science—History—20th century. 2. Technology—History—20th century.]
Q126.4.Y43 1995
609'.04—dc20   95–17485
                                                                     CIP
                                                                      AC

ISBN 0–8050–3433–1
First Edition 1995
Printed in Mexico
All first editions are printed on acid-free paper ∞.
10 9 8 7 6 5 4 3 2 1

Cover design by James Sinclair
Interior design by Kelly Soong

Cover photo credits
Background: Empire State Building, © Townsend P. Dickinson/Comstock. **Inset images** (clockwise from right), symbol for the planet Pluto; radio telescope, © 1994 David Lawrence/The Stock Market; streptococcus bacteria, © David Phillips/Photo Researchers, Inc.; "hole" in ozone layer over Antarctica, NASA/Science Photo Library/Photo Researchers, Inc.; computer-generated image of vitamin C, © 1993 Dan Richardson/ Medichrome; MRI brain scan, Mehau Kulyk/SPL/Photo Researchers, Inc.

Photo Credits
p.10: Neg./Trans. No. 3143 (Photo by Shuppan)/Courtesy Department of Library Services, American Museum of Natural History; p.14(top & bottom): Courtesy of Dupont Corporation; p.16: Archive Photos/Ewing Krainin; p.17: NASA/Science Photo Library/Photo Researchers, Inc.; p.22, 25, 29, 37, 63, 71: UPI/Bettmann; p.24: NASA; p.32: The MIT Museum; p.33: Courtesy of IBM Corporation; p.36: The Bettmann Archive; p.43: Ted Horowitz/The Stock Market; p.44: Mehau Kulyk/SPL/Photo Researchers, Inc.; p. 46 (top): Golden Gate Bridge, Highway & Transportation District Archives; p.46 (bottom): Bruce Hands/© Tony Stone Images; p.48: Lowell Georgia/Science Source/Photo Researchers, Inc.; p.49: Courtesy of Owens Fiberglass; p.52: Lowell Observatory; p.54: © 1994 David Lawrence/The Stock Market; p.55, 67 (top): SPL/Photo Researchers, Inc.; p.59: © Michael Siegel/Phototake, NYC; p.62: Dr. Jeremy Burgess/SPL/Photo Researchers, Inc.; p.67 (bottom) Lawrence Berkeley Laboratory/SPL/Photo Researchers, Inc.

To John Bale

Contents

Introduction

DAWN OF THE SCIENTIFIC EXPLOSION

History books reveal the 1930s as a grim decade during which the wealthiest countries in the world began spinning dangerously out of control. This was the era of the great worldwide economic depression, when the price of agricultural products collapsed, investors lost fortunes, banks failed, and millions of able-bodied laborers were thrown out of work. It was a decade of political unrest that spawned the hideous Nazi government of Germany and ended in a brutal war that spread throughout much of the world.

All of this clamor and chaos drowned out the amazing explosion that took place during the 1930s in science and technology. The fuse for this explosion was lit during World War I, when governments began to recognize the enormous potential of science and technology to deliver a military advantage. During the 1920s, governments concerned about the security of their nations began pouring money into research and development. Large corporations also began to see that research could pay huge dividends in creating new products or in gaining an advantage over competitors. Many scientific advances then had a domino effect—one new discovery opened the door to a thousand other new possibilities.

The explosion of scientific information in the 1930s often caught even the experts by surprise. In December of 1935, a trawler fishing off the coast of South Africa hauled in an odd-looking 5-foot- (1.5-meter-) long fish. Instead of being attached directly to its body, the fish's fins were connected to fleshy lobes that looked something like stubby arms. South African zoologist J. L. B. Smith identified the fish as a coelacanth. The announcement astounded experts throughout the world as much as if Smith had declared he had captured a living dinosaur. For the coelacanth was a primitive species of fish that lived among the dinosaurs and was thought to have been extinct for seventy million years.

A coelacanth, a primitive fish belonging to a species thought to have been extinct for millions of years, was discovered alive in 1935.

Other surprises with a greater impact on everyday life lay in wait in the 1930s. Engineers calculated that the jet propulsion engine could never produce enough thrust to be of any practical use in flight. Yet even while the experts were completing their negative reports, jet fighter planes roared over the skies of Germany at record speeds.

Few people knew what to make of the recently discovered existence of radioactivity. Many considered this puzzling phenomenon a fascinating new toy that could possibly produce revolutionary health cures. At the start of the 1930s, a pharmaceutical manual listed nearly one hundred medicines that had been laced with radioactive ingredients. Consumers could even buy radioactive chocolate bars and toothpaste! Stunning new information on radioactivity came to light during the 1930s as scientists unraveled the deadly secrets of this new fad.

Meanwhile, the foremost physicist of his time, Ernest Rutherford, declared that the notion of harnessing the power of the atomic nucleus was nothing more than "moonshine." But by the end of the 1930s, physicists would uncover truths about the power of atoms that would rock the world and cast a menacing shadow over the world for all time to come.

As the 1930s unfolded, medical doctors looked on helplessly while diseases such as malaria and typhus claimed victims by the millions and while fatal infections raged through human bodies. The idea that substances existed that could kill infectious bacteria without seriously damaging the host they lived in seemed a wild fantasy. Yet by the end of the decade, medical science would go on a rampage, attacking infectious diseases with a huge arsenal of new drugs, conjuring up dreams of a future world completely without disease.

At the beginning of the 1930s, humans depended entirely on nature to supply the raw materials for clothing, shelter, and consumer goods. Some of these materials, such as silk, were in short supply. Others contained flaws that hampered their effectiveness. Wood rotted, iron rusted, glass broke easily. These weaknesses put limits on humans' ability to construct desired items. By the end of the decade, however, a person could be covered from head to foot in material created artificially in laboratories. Engineers and inventors had an entirely new family of materials—plastics—with which to design new products and structures.

Prior to the decade of the 1930s, people had never probed more than a few hundred feet below the earth's surface. They had never ventured into the stratosphere that surrounds the earth. The scientific explosion of the 1930s quickly blew away these last frontiers on the planet. Astronomers came up with mind-boggling calculations describing cosmic matter so dense that it erased all previous concepts of the form that matter could take.

Most importantly, science and technology began to shape society as they had never done before. Scientific discoveries in the 1930s brought forth new products on an almost daily basis. From awesome atom smashers and miracle medicines to trivial innovations such as the beer can, a practical ballpoint pen, and sliced bread, the decade heaped innovation upon innovation. Science and technology accelerated the pace of life by speeding up travel and communication. Researchers flooded the market with choices. They eliminated work by creating devices that would automatically accomplish tasks that people once did for themselves. They altered climate so that people could live in cool comfort and keep food refrigerated, even frozen, during oppressive heat waves.

At the beginning of the decade, few people could imagine that they would soon be flying in comfort at high altitudes in pressurized cabins. Few could expect that they would be reading books with paperback covers in the soft glow of fluorescent lighting. Nor would they have expected a household in which blenders, can openers, and knives were run by electricity. The notion of affordable machines that could take over the drudgery of washing clothes and dishes was a wistful fantasy.

The explosion of scientific information that accelerated in the 1930s held one last surprise for the curious dabblers who invoked its magic. Just when people began, for the first time, to *expect* science and technology to solve problems that came up, to improve their lives, they began to see signs that there was a price to pay for following science's lead. Science and technology could provide remarkable solutions to problems, but at the same time they introduced new dangers that society sixty years later is only beginning to understand.

1

CHEMISTRY

Ever since Leo H. Baekeland mixed phenol, formaldehyde, and bases in 1907 to create a durable plastic substance, chemists have been busy creating artificial materials. In the words of C.M.A. Stine of the Du Pont Corporation, Baekeland's discovery led us "to view wood, metal, fiber, rubber, and all other natural products not as raw materials in themselves, but as compounds of raw materials that are ever present in air, water and soil."

SYNTHETIC MATERIALS

In the 1930s, chemists took hold of this idea to reshape society. Wallace H. Carothers, a research chemist at the Du Pont chemical company, made one of the most important discoveries while working with giant molecules called polymers. The study of polymers, which are formed by combining two or more molecules into long chains, was such a new field in 1930 that some chemists refused to believe these molecules existed.

Carothers directed a research effort aimed at making artificial polymers. In 1931, he combined adipic acid with hexamethylene diamine to form the world's first artificial fiber, which he called nylon. These first nylon fibers were formed by a process in which the removal of water from the chemical solution caused individual molecules to join together. The nylon produced in this way was too flimsy to be of any use. Carothers and his team found that this was because the water fell back into solution and upset the process. Once they perfected a way to channel water out of the system in 1935, they produced an extremely tough material. They then found a way to create nylon threads by melting the nylon material and forcing it through spinnerettes.

Above: *A colleague of Wallace Carothers reenacts the discovery of nylon—the first artificial fiber.*

Right: *Kitchen utensils coated with Teflon have become common since the discovery of polytetrafluoroethylene in the 1930s.*

Nylon proved to be a wonderful substitute for silk—an expensive and relatively rare protein fiber produced by silkworms. Since nylon was produced by chemical materials that came from abundant substances—coal, air, and water—it could be produced far more cheaply without any fears of a shortage. In addition to these qualities, nylon was elastic, stronger than silk, and it resisted grease, dirt, and mildew. It did not shrink, and it would not be eaten by moths. Nylon could be used for a variety of products from stylish clothing to toothbrush bristles to fishing lines.

Few commercial products have enjoyed the instant success of nylon stockings. They were introduced in 1938, and sixty-four million pairs were sold in that first year.

Nylon kicked off an explosion in synthetic textiles. By the end of the decade, a person could be decked out from head to foot in materials created entirely in a laboratory. Chemists created thousands of new plastic materials that eliminated the shortcomings of natural products. They created wood substitutes that did not rot, metal substitutes that did not rust, glass substitutes that did not break. During the 1930s, chemical laboratories splashed the world in color by cranking out hundreds of thousands of new chemical dyes. They improved the availability of electrical products by creating insulators such as polyvinyl chloride and polystyrene. They eased the drudgery of kitchen cleanup by introducing the polymer polytetrafluoroethylene, commonly known as Teflon, to create nonstick fry pans. Chemists improved packaging possibilities by discovering durable materials such as polyethylene. They learned how to artificially produce costly natural scents such as rare musk oil for a tiny fraction of the cost.

KEEPING THINGS COOL

Chemists also changed society by improving humans' ability to control temperature. In previous decades, scientists and engineers had discovered how to cool small amounts of air by using liquids that evaporate easily. This cooling occurs because a liquid loses some of its heat when it turns to vapor. Engineers used this principle to build devices that drew heat from the surrounding environment to replace the heat lost by the evaporating liquid. This was the basis of the refrigerator and air conditioner.

Prior to the 1930s, however, the refrigerants used to provide the cooling effect were highly poisonous and unstable. These substances could leak out of the system and produce foul odors, choking, and even death. As a result, few products made use of the ability to cool air. Virtually all refrigeration of food was done the old-fashioned way—with ice chests, which had to be frequently reloaded with fresh ice to replace the ice that melted.

That changed in 1930 when American chemist Thomas Midgley Jr. discovered the cooling properties of chlorofluoromethane, whose molecules consist of a carbon atom plus two fluorine atoms and two chlorine atoms. This substance not only evaporated easily, but was safe to use, stable, odorless, and affordable. In 1931, the Kinetic Chemical Corporation began manufacturing this substance under the name Freon.

Almost as soon as Freon hit the market, it changed the lifestyle of American society. Freon-cooled refrigerators became common in households in the 1930s. This led to the public acceptance of frozen foods, which

Here's a look inside a Freon-cooled refrigerator.

had been introduced by Clarence Birdseye in the 1920s. By the end of the decade, Freon-based air conditioners were even being installed in automobiles. Use of air conditioners in industrialized countries has mushroomed ever since, allowing people to drive, shop, work, play, and sleep in a comfortable, temperature-controlled environment.

In 1921, manufacturers in the United States produced only 5,000 refrigerators. Thanks to the improvements provided by Freon, that number jumped to thirty-seven *million* in 1937.

PAYING THE PRICE FOR PROGRESS

But while Freon took the danger out of refrigeration and air-conditioning, it also introduced a more deadly danger that has only recently been discovered. Scientists have been alarmed at the disintegration of ozone in the earth's atmosphere. Ozone is a form of oxygen that forms a thin layer protecting the earth from the sun's harmful rays. Loss of that ozone protection could mean disastrous consequences for the earth, including increased occurrence of cancer and decreased plant production. Recent evidence has pointed to Freon as one of the prime causes of ozone destruction.

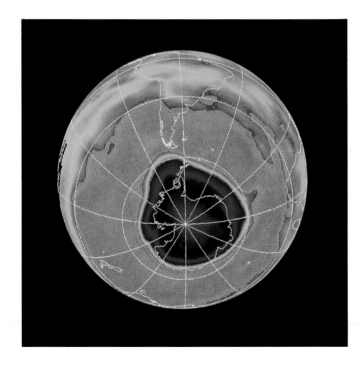

A satellite map shows a "hole" in the ozone layer over Antarctica in 1990. Scientists of the 1930s were unaware of the problems Freon could cause, including ozone destruction.

A similar tale of a 1930s triumph gone sour involves the chemical DDT. By the twentieth century, scientists had determined that insects were not merely irritating nuisances but were actually more dangerous to humans than any other creatures. Body lice, for example, carry the disease typhus, which killed far more people during World War I than actual combat. More than five million Russians alone died from typhus in the five years following that war. At the same time, malaria, transmitted by mosquitoes, was infecting more than one hundred million people worldwide each year, causing three million deaths per year. Mosquitoes also spread misery in the forms of yellow fever and encephalitis. Other insects produced famine by destroying crops in the field.

Swiss chemist Paul Müller was among those scientists recruited to launch a war against insects. Working for the J. R. Geigy company, he searched for a substance that could kill insects without harming other forms of life.

Müller quickly determined that the most effective poisons against insects were those that killed on contact rather than those that insects had to ingest (eat). Contact poisons needed to be stable so that they would last long enough to ensure contact with the insect.

One synthetic substance that met both requirements was dichloro-diphenyltrichloroethane, or DDT for short. DDT had been available since 1874, but no one had previously recognized its value as an insecticide. In the late 1930s, Müller found that DDT killed many kinds of insects without any apparent harmful effect on other creatures. Since it was made from the common materials of chlorine, alcohol, and sulfuric acid, it could be made inexpensively in large quantities. Furthermore, DDT was odorless and light-weight for easy transportation.

Müller knew he had a potent product when the effects of DDT lingered even after he tried to clean up his experiment. Flies continued to fall dead when they touched walls that Müller thought had been thoroughly cleansed of DDT.

DDT immediately revolutionized public health. It saved millions of lives around the world, particularly following World War II, when it prevented the expected devastating typhus outbreaks. DDT's effect on mosquitoes dramatically reduced malaria incidences around the world. It made previously uninhabitable marshlands safe for people to live in and it protected croplands from devastation.

Eventually, however, the miracle of DDT proved to be a mixed blessing at best. The chemical turned out to be more harmful to invertebrates, fish, and mammals than was first believed. The fact that it lingered in the environment made it difficult to stop long-term damage once the poison was released into the environment. DDT also caused a ripple effect of devastation in the food chain. Elimination of insects robbed insect eaters of their food and caused a decline in the numbers of these animals. This eliminated natural control of pests. Since insects reproduce rapidly, they were able to evolve immunities to DDT in a relatively short period of time. This turned the tables on the chemical. Now, instead of being harmful to insects and harmless to other creatures, lingering DDT was harming other creatures and showing a limited effect against insects. Once the broad effects of DDT became known, the United States government banned the use of the chemical except in special cases.

The experience with DDT eventually led to a new awareness of the impact of human activity on the environment. The 1930s also sowed the seeds of another environmental controversy with the findings of G. S. Callendar. In 1938, Callendar reported that humans' use of energy was increasing the level of carbon dioxide in the earth's atmosphere. This was the first warning of the existence of the greenhouse effect, something that could produce global warming. Global warming also raised the possibility that peoples' disregard of the environment could have catastrophic effects on the future of the planet.

2

TRANSPORTATION

Prior to the 1930s, the ocean was a gigantic, mysterious black box. No one could go down to see what was happening in its murky depths. Crude submarines and diving suits could carry people beneath the surface of the ocean. But the pressure of the sea increased its crushing grip with every foot of depth. No diving suit or submarine hull could withstand the pressure beyond a few hundred feet. Sailors could get samples of what lived down in the unlighted waters only by pulling up creatures that happened to get tangled in their longest nets, which measured nearly 2 miles (3.2 kilometers).

MYSTERIES OF THE DEEP

The curious dead specimens hauled in by nets sparked the curiosity of American naturalist Charles Beebe. Along with Otis Barton, Beebe designed a small steel sphere powerful enough to withstand the overwhelming pressures of the sea. Thick windows made of polished quartz rock gave him an 8-inch (20-centimeter) observation porthole through which he could look out on the previously unseen world. Beebe called his vessel a bathysphere, from Greek words meaning "sphere of the deep."

On June 6, 1930, a ship transported Beebe, Barton, and the bathysphere to a spot 10 miles (16 kilometers) south of Bermuda in the Caribbean Sea for the first dive. The enormity of what he was about to do struck Beebe speechless. "Not being able to think of any pithy saying which might echo down the ages, I said nothing," Beebe admitted. Silently, he crawled in. Barton joined him in the cramped 4.5-foot- (1.4-meter-) diameter compartment.

Steel cables lowered them into the water. Beebe communicated with the ship's operators through a solid rubber hose that contained both telephone and electrical wires. With the hissing of oxygen tanks around him, Beebe

Charles Beebe (right) *and Otis Barton* (left) *prepare for a descent in the bathysphere.*

peered out as the cables lowered them to 800 feet (244 meters), deeper than any human had probed before.

"I was looking toward a world of life almost as unknown as that of Venus or Mars," Beebe reported. He provided a running commentary to those above, describing the fish and the inky blue color of the ocean.

Beebe and Barton took an incredible risk with their untested system. Had the cables broken, there was no backup system to save them. They simply would have sunk to the bottom, never to return. Yet the men seemed too excited to notice the danger. When their hatch began leaking water at 300 feet (91 meters), they refused to call off the trial. They counted on the increased pressure of the water to seal the door more tightly as they went deeper. Fortunately, they were right.

Five days later, Beebe and Barton took the bathysphere to an even greater depth, nearly a quarter mile, or 1,320 feet (400 meters), below the surface. For the first time, a human witnessed electric fish and squid swimming in their deep sea domain. Beebe felt like "an infinitesimal atom floating in illimitable space."

With improved equipment, Beebe and Barton continued to extend their probes into the ocean depths. In 1934, they descended to 3,028 feet (923 meters) below the surface of the water, shedding light on a previously unseen part of life on earth.

EXPLORING THE ATMOSPHERE

While Beebe was documenting life in the depths, others were exploring the heights far above the earth. Auguste Piccard, a professor at the University of Brussels in Belgium, built a hot-air balloon equipped with a sealed aluminum cabin in the gondola. He hoped that this would help him survive the frigid temperatures and lack of air in the stratosphere—the cloudless upper level of the atmosphere.

Piccard had to call off his first attempt to reach the stratosphere because of high winds that picked up just as he was rising off the ground. The press had a field day ridiculing the fiasco. The story got around that Piccard was an absentminded professor who had made such a huge blunder in his calculations that his balloon reached only 10 feet (3 meters) rather than the expected 10 miles (16 kilometers).

On May 27, 1931, Piccard answered his critics by successfully launching his balloon. As he rose ever higher into the sky, the supposedly airtight cabin soon sprouted a leak. Furthermore, Piccard's attempt to regulate the cabin's heat by painting one side of the gondola black failed because he lost the ability to turn the craft. Because of this, the black side continually faced the sun and absorbed the sun's rays, unblocked by atmosphere. Despite a surrounding atmospheric temperature of -76°F (-60°C), Piccard was broiling in the sun. Nevertheless, he climbed to a height of almost 10 miles (16 kilometers), higher than anyone had gone before. (Four years later, Albert Stevens of the United States sailed a balloon even higher, to 13.7 miles [22 kilometers] above sea level. From there, he took a photograph that covered an area equal to the state of Indiana, by far the largest area ever photographed at once.)

Piccard was not simply sightseeing in the bluish purple radiance of the stratosphere. He was curious about the makeup of the gases that compose this region. Piccard took with him instruments that could measure the amount of ozone, the special form of oxygen that forms a thin protective blanket over the atmosphere and shields earth's inhabitants from the sun's harmful ultraviolet radiation.

Piccard was also interested in finding out more about the cosmic radiation that scientists had recorded coming from outer space. His measurements revealed that the atmosphere absorbed most of the less penetrating radiation but that some radiation was actually produced in the atmosphere.

Stratospheric measurements of the type that Piccard made have since become common. Among their most important findings is that the ozone layer that Piccard examined is being destroyed, probably as a result of human activity.

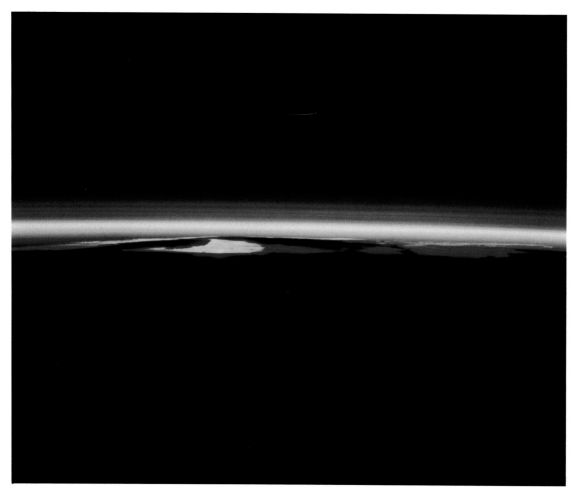

This image, taken from space, shows how thin earth's atmosphere is. Black areas in the photograph are the unlit earth in the foreground, and the darkness of space, above the atmosphere.

THE NEED FOR SPEED

Some scientists and inventors were not interested in where they could go as much as how fast they could get there. Several of them toyed with the principle first expressed by Sir Isaac Newton in 1687, that to every action there is an equal and opposite reaction. This principle offered the hope of producing high-speed projectiles or craft powered by an explosive discharge of gases. If the discharge was aimed to the rear, the equal and opposite reaction should propel the craft forward.

During the 1910s and 1920s, Robert Goddard, a professor at Clark College in Worcester, Massachusetts, had been tinkering with this notion in his work on rockets. The main obstacle that stood in the way of rocket development was the difficulty of harnessing such explosive discharges so that the speed and direction of the craft could be controlled. Despite the scorn of his critics, Goddard had succeeded in creating a combustion chamber and exhaust nozzle that used the power of liquid oxygen and gasoline to propel his rocket at high speed.

Robert Goddard, with one of his earliest rockets

Goddard's research was temporarily derailed by a local fire marshal. Responding to reports of a downed airplane in 1929, local authorities rushed police and medical help to the scene of the accident. Instead of an airplane, they found one of Goddard's rockets. The irate fire marshal banned Goddard from further rocket launchings. Eventually, Goddard moved to a barren section of New Mexico to continue his work.

During the 1930s, Goddard continued his lonely quest to perfect the rocket. By 1935, he had fired a rocket that traveled faster than the speed of sound to a height of 9,000 feet (2,740 meters).

Goddard saw that his research was providing a way to launch explorations into space. Unfortunately, he never could interest fellow scientists, the American government, or the public in what he was doing. Shortly before his death in 1945, he wrote, "The subject of projection from the earth, and especially mention of the moon, must still be avoided in dignified scientific and engineering circles." Only long after his death did the American government take advantage of Goddard's findings to launch a successful space exploration program that included Goddard's dream of landing a person on the moon.

GERMAN ROCKET RESEARCH

While Goddard could not convince those around him of the importance of his work, the German government took a careful look at his rocket research. At first the Germans were interested in rockets as a means to boost heavily loaded aircraft into the air. But soon they began to see possibilities for both high-speed aircraft and long-range missiles. In the mid-1930s, they poured money into a large rocket research station on the Baltic Sea. The rocket research team, led by physicist Wernher Von Braun, courted constant danger as they tried to find a way to manage the explosive hydrogen peroxide that they used as fuel. The unstable fuel blew entire buildings to splinters. In 1936, Von Braun's first two remote-controlled test flights of rocket-powered fighter planes ended in disaster—the planes exploded on takeoff. In March of the following year, Erich Warsitz had barely started down the runway in his first attempt to fly a rocket-powered Heinkel fighter when it exploded.

Warsitz survived the mishap and one month later tried again. He took off under conventional gasoline propeller power. When he reached 2,600 feet (792 meters), he fired up the rocket engine. Warsitz reported that he felt as though he had been "kicked in the backside." His plane shot forward, carrying Warsitz on an exhilarating thirty-second ride. The Heinkel Company then designed and built the He 176, a plane driven solely by rocket power. Although Warsitz successfully flew the plane in 1939, Germany began to lose interest in rocket-powered fighters. Instead it turned its focus to explosive missiles. Before the 1930s were over, Von Braun was well on his way to perfecting the V-2. This rocket-powered missile could travel faster than the speed of sound, which enabled it to carry 1,600 pounds (725 kilograms) of explosives to a target 200 miles (320 kilometers) away with virtually no warning.

Had Von Braun completed his work a couple of years earlier, the Germans might have had a decisive military advantage in World War II. The pioneering efforts of Goddard and Von Braun paved the way for future space flights as well as nuclear missiles with a range of thousands of miles.

ANOTHER BREAKTHROUGH IN HIGH-SPEED FLIGHT

The principle of propelling objects forward with a high-powered discharge led to the development of another breakthrough in high-speed flight—the jet engine. In the 1920s, Frank Whittle, a teenage student at the Royal Air Force College in Great Britain, had begun experiments in jet propulsion. Jet propulsion differs from rocket propulsion in that it relies on a high volume of compressed air and continuous, steady fuel burning, rather than explosive burning to provide the rear discharge.

Others had probed the possibilities of jet engines in the past. Henri Coanda of Romania had even built a jet engine prototype in 1910, but it was not practical. The tremendous heat produced by the mixture of compressed air and burning gas quickly destroyed the engine.

In 1930, Whittle found a way to make the jet concept workable for an engine. He funneled the jet gases from the heating of compressed air and fuel into a turbine. The hot gases spun the turbine, which provided the power that drove the plane. The concept of jet power was appealing because it was safer than rocket power. It could provide greater power than a conventional propeller-driven plane with a much smaller, lighter engine. This would allow planes to travel at higher speeds. But there remained the problem of heat production. Metal simply could not withstand the heat thrown off by the jet. The British government believed this defect made the whole plan impractical, and it failed to support Whittle's turbojet research even after he was awarded his patents.

During the early 1930s, however, new metal alloys became available that *could* stand up to extremely high temperatures. Using these materials, Whittle built a practical jet engine in 1937. But while he was working on this, Germany was following up on the success of engineer Hans von Ohain, who developed his own jet engine in 1939. The German government was quicker than the British to see the military advantages to a jet aircraft. The Germans were aware that piston-driven aircraft were reaching the limits of their abilities. A jet-powered aircraft would not be bound by those limits and could make possible a much faster, higher-altitude plane.

Backed by the German government, the Heinkel Company developed an experimental jet fighter, the He 178. On August 27, 1939, the fearless Erich Warsitz roared off the runway at Marienke, Germany, and flew the He 178 on a six-minute flight. Jet-powered flight had become a reality. Great Britain belatedly stepped up its jet airplane research. By the end of World War II, both Germany and Great Britain were flying jet fighters.

ROTARY-WING FLIGHT

While speed proved to be an important benefit in air flight, it presented a problem. Airplanes designed for speed required long runways and wide-open areas for takeoff and landing. This meant that air flight could be of no benefit in transporting people and materials to places that did not have such open spaces, particularly cities.

The idea of an aircraft that could rise straight up from an enclosed space became especially attractive. The obvious way to design such a craft was to put a propeller on top to pull the vehicle up, rather than in the front to pull it forward. But putting this simple concept into practice proved difficult. Such inventive geniuses as Thomas Edison and Alexander Graham Bell tried to solve the mystery of rotary-wing flight, without success.

Actually, an Italian helicopter beat the Wright brothers' first airplane into the air by twenty-five years. The name *helicopter* comes from two Greek words meaning "helical (spiral) wing." It hovered for about twenty seconds at a height of nearly 40 feet (12 meters). The helicopter was too difficult to control, however, and so its development stopped in its tracks while airplane advances proceeded rapidly.

In the mid-1930s, the French conducted successful trials of their own helicopter prototype, one of which covered more than 27 miles (43 kilometers) during a flight that lasted more than an hour. But they were unable to work out design problems well enough to get a product on the market.

German engineer Heinrich Focke finally achieved a practical design in 1936. His version of the helicopter flew 143 miles (230 kilometers) at a speed of more than 76 miles (122 kilometers) per hour in 1937. But even though several of these were eventually used by Germany in World War II, this model failed to win widespread acceptance.

The helicopter did not become a familiar part of air travel until Russian-born American engineer Igor Sikorsky completed his thirty-year effort to build a helicopter. Sikorsky had been designing and building toy helicopters

Igor Sikorsky prepares to test an early version of the helicopter.

since he was twelve. "I was sure that an aircraft that could fly like a hummingbird would be immensely useful," he said.

His first serious attempt in 1909 ended in failure. Sikorsky realized that the technology and proper materials for constructing such an aircraft were not yet available. He set aside his plans for the helicopter and worked on other aeronautical projects, such as building the world's first multiengine airplane in 1913.

Following the Russian Revolution in 1917, Sikorsky moved to the United States. He continued to work on airplanes and formed his own aircraft construction company, all the while taking notes and sketching out designs for a helicopter. At last, in early 1939, he felt he had the technology and materials to achieve his lifelong dream. At his factory in Stratford, Connecticut, he began to put together his VS-300.

By fall, the first helicopter was complete. Sikorsky used a three-blade main rotor over the top of the craft, with blades 28 feet (8.5 meters) in diameter to provide the power. He achieved stability by adding a small rotor at the rear to prevent the fuselage from rotating.

Sikorsky was always the first to take the controls of anything he designed. On September 14, 1939, he lifted his VS-300 into the air on a short but successful run. He could take off straight up into the air and land the same way. The VS-300 could fly forward or backward or could hover in one spot, depending on how Sikorsky set the pitch of the rotors.

Sikorsky's model was the first helicopter useful and practical enough to go into mass production. American forces used about 400 of them during World War II. Helicopters have become immensely useful for many tasks airplanes cannot handle, including search and rescue missions, troop transport, ambulance transport, wilderness mapping, and hauling workers and equipment to places that have difficult access—such as offshore oil rigs. The design that Sikorsky developed in 1939 is still the basis for helicopters built today.

3

COMMUNICATION AND INFORMATION

The greatest scientific breakthroughs in the 1930s in communication and information processing had absolutely no effect on the average person of that era. But the seeds of computers, television, and photocopiers that scientists sowed during that time would eventually blossom twenty, thirty, and forty years later. They have flourished so well that it is now hard to imagine life without these technologies.

INFORMATION MACHINES

The notion of an automatic calculating machine had advanced in fits and spasms for more than a century. Charles Babbage from England had laid grandiose plans to build such a machine back in the early nineteenth century, but without much success. Various individuals and companies later focused on more realistic goals. They created small tabulating machines that could solve a limited range of arithmetic problems. Unfortunately, thousands of moving parts were required for even simple machines. With so many mechanical parts involved, the processes were slow and the machines were subject to breakdowns.

The vacuum tubes and electronic circuits developed in the 1920s provided a way of eliminating much of this cumbersome machinery. One of the first to make use of this was Daniel Woodbury, an electrical engineering student at the Massachusetts Institute of Technology, who was working on his master's thesis in 1922. Realizing that his thesis required reams of mind-numbing calculations, Woodbury invented a small machine that could do the work. When his adviser, Vannevar Bush, found out what Woodbury had built, he said, "Give up all that slip-stick work and write us a thesis on your invention."

*Vannevar Bush
with the Differential
Analyzer*

Woodbury's creation led to the development of Bush's Differential
Analyzer, a partially electronic computer. This machine could handle as
many as eighteen independent variables and could be programmed to solve a
number of the tedious complex equations that continually bogged down scientists in their research.

Setting up the machine to solve a particular problem, however, was a difficult, time-consuming task. In 1935, Bush and his team began to incorporate
the idea of punch tape, translating information into a pattern of holes on a
card or tape and feeding it into the machine.

Encouraged by the success of his machine, Bush sketched out plans for
an even more complex and efficient Rapid Arithmetical Machine in 1937. But
research demands prompted by World War II prevented him from working on
the project.

In the meantime, others had taken up the challenge of computers.
Americans John Atanasoff and Clifford Berry built a prototype electronic
computer in 1937. But frequent breakdowns limited its usefulness. Across
the Atlantic Ocean, Great Britain's Alan Turing was exploring the concept of
building intelligence into machines. In 1936, he proved mathematically that
machines could be taught artificial intelligence. Shortly thereafter, he began

work on an electronic computer. His team created a machine capable of mathematically breaking down Germany's top secret Enigma military codes. This would eventually provide the British with a crucial edge in their fight for survival against Nazi Germany.

DAWN OF THE COMPUTER AGE

Perhaps the man most responsible for advancing computer technology was a Harvard graduate student in physics, Howard Aiken. Like Daniel Woodbury, Aiken found himself slaving away for hundreds of hours at complex but routine calculations during his research. Some of the information he wanted required calculations too complex and time-consuming to be worth anyone's time. Aiken dreamed of building a machine that could perform the task quickly and efficiently.

In 1937, he outlined a plan for a Proposed Automatic Calculating Machine, which could solve practically any mathematical problem, no matter how complex, within a reasonable amount of time. Aiken's academic advisers at Harvard joined business professionals in belittling Aiken's pro-

The IBM Automatic Sequence Controlled Calculator shows how enormous early computers were.

Early computers were sprawling monsters. Vannevar Bush's early machines used 2,000 electron tubes, 200 miles (322 kilometers) of wire, and 150 motors weighing a total of 100 tons (90 metric tons). Howard Aiken's Mark I was 51 feet (15.5 meters) long and contained nearly three-quarters of a million parts, 175,000 electrical connections, and 530 miles (855 kilometers) of wire.

posal. But Aiken hooked up with International Business Machines (IBM), a small young company with a track record of creative improvements in punch card-operated calculating machines. IBM saw possibilities in Aiken's notion and took the bold step of joining with Harvard to fund a research effort to build Aiken's machine.

Aiken and IBM did not produce a computer during the 1930s. But their efforts throughout this decade cleared away enough obstacles so that the Mark I computer was up and running by 1944. This electronically controlled machine could multiply eleven-digit numbers in three seconds, far exceeding the skill of most mathematicians. Once the innovators of the 1930s demonstrated the concept of electronic computers, all that remained was for those who followed to compete in designing faster, smaller, and more powerful versions.

Copy After Copy After Copy

Another technological advance that has revolutionized the modern office, photocopying, also germinated in the 1930s. This was the brainchild of Chester Carlson, a shy, serious young man working in the patents department of a company that made electrical components. Patent applications often required Carlson to submit duplicates of documents. This was no great problem for manuscript pages—providing one knew ahead of time what needed to be copied. A person could simply slip a sheet of carbon paper between sheets of typing paper and type the duplicate along with the original. But if the paper included drawings, as patent applications often do, or was already typed, the entire document would have to be redone. Carlson, whose poor eyesight made such time-consuming paperwork all the more difficult, wondered if there was a better way to create copies.

Researching the topic in his spare time in the New York Public Library, Carlson came across information on photoconductivity. He read about how small metal particles could be attracted to points on a surface that were electrically charged by means of static electricity. If particles could be attracted to certain points, he thought, they could be attracted to points that were in the shape of letters and other images.

Strapped for cash, Carlson performed his experiments on makeshift equipment in his apartment in Queens, New York. He found that chemical powders clinging to electrically charged metal plates would lose their attraction if he exposed the plates to light. This provided a means of getting the powder to take the forms he wanted. All he had to do was expose a charged plate full of powder to light but shield the parts on which he wanted powder to remain. The powder on the portions of the plate that were exposed to light would fall off, leaving powder only on the unexposed part.

> Carlson often used foul-smelling sulfur in his experiments. One night his landlord's daughter came up to complain about the reek. So it was that the loner, Carlson, met his future wife.

Carlson got a patent for his idea in 1937 but continued to struggle to find a way to actually make a workable copier. One day he printed the date, October 22, 1938, and the name of his neighborhood, Astoria, in pen on a glass slide. Carlson pressed this slide against a charged metal plate and held the two pieces together up to the light. The ink figures blocked the light from striking the part of the plate directly under them.

Carlson removed the slide and spread powder on the plate. He then pressed waxed paper over the plate and heated it. Turning over the paper, he blew loose the excess powder and saw "10-22-38 Astoria" printed on it.

There remained the problem of designing an affordable machine that could do this copying simply and cheaply. Carlson would spend ten more years working on the problem before anyone took him seriously, followed by another ten years before a practical version of his copier came on the market. Photocopying would not revolutionize office work around the world until the 1960s and 1970s. Nonetheless, Carlson's discovery belonged to the 1930s.

Chester Carlson worked for years before his copier became available on the market.

TELEVISION COMES INTO FOCUS

On the other hand, the 1930s was the decade in which groundwork laid for the television in earlier decades finally began to pay off. By 1930, Scotsman John Baird had produced a television that provided a fuzzy image on the screen. He sold about 1,000 sets. British racing fans were also able to watch a horse race on closed-circuit television in 1931.

Meanwhile, Vladimir Zworykin, a Russian engineer who had immigrated to the United States in 1919, was hard at work on his own television design. Back in 1923, Zworykin's employer had told him to quit wasting his time on his notion of an all-electric system that could transmit clear, live images onto a screen. But in 1930, Zworykin found a company, Radio Corporation of America (RCA), willing to back his venture.

Zworykin's system used a camera that translated different light intensities into varying electronic currents. Then a receiver would convert the electronic current back into the corresponding brightness of light and would produce an image on screen.

The more photosensitive (sensitive to light) spots available to record the difference in light intensity, the clearer the picture would be. Zworykin found that by pouring silver oxide powder onto a sheet of mica and then heating it, he could produce millions of tiny silver specks, each separately insulated by mica. Zworykin treated the silver with cesium oxide to make it photosensitive. As a light beam scanned these light receptors, each would emit electrons in proportion to the brightness of the light. Zworykin then designed a television screen that could store the varying light intensities at each point of the image and electronically re-create the image on a screen.

In 1932, RCA conducted a test of Zworykin's system against other television methods being developed. Zworykin's system won easily. In 1933, RCA ran a field test, broadcasting a picture from a television camera to a televi-

Vladimir Zworykin's work refining his television design spanned several decades.

sion receiver 4 miles (6.4 kilometers) away. Using techniques developed by the radio industry for amplifying electronic signals, RCA technicians eventually designed a commercial television that could receive pictures from hundreds of miles away.

Government regulations and the chaos of World War II delayed the production of commercial television in the United States until the mid-1940s. But the practicality of the concept had been confirmed before the 1930s ended. Vladimir Zworykin's invention was primed to give people access to sights and information they would never otherwise have seen and, for better or worse, to drastically change lifestyles around the world.

SEEING RED

Technicolor provided another improvement in visual communication. Prior to the 1930s, motion picture producers had no satisfactory way of creating color motion pictures. They had attempted to bring color into the theater even before the twentieth century, by coloring each frame of film by hand. Since that time, mechanical stencils had been developed to speed up the process, but it remained a tedious and overwhelming task.

The process of technicolor used a special movie camera that created three film negatives at once—in red, blue, and green. These negatives were developed and the colors were then transferred onto a blank film. Walt Disney was the first to use technicolor, in a 1932 cartoon called *Flowers and Trees*. He first used the process in a full-length motion picture in 1935. Before long, virtually all studios were using the technicolor process.

RECORDING AND BROADCASTING SOUND

While the television and technicolor were improving society's access to images, the tape recorder improved access to sound. Magnetized metal provided the means of storage. In 1929, Fritz Pfleumer of Germany won a patent for his novel idea of using a flexible plastic tape coated with magnetic material to record sound. German companies perfected the concept in the 1930s, using tape dusted with magnetic iron dioxide. The person who made the best initial use of the tape recorder was Nazi leader Adolf Hitler. His entire speeches were often tape-recorded and rebroadcast throughout Germany.

With the clarity of these recordings, Germans had no problem hearing what Hitler wanted to say. Unlike most inventors, who quickly export their new devices to the world, the Germans kept a tight lid on their tape recording technology and it did not become widely used outside Germany until after World War II.

Another 1930s milestone in sound communication was Edward Armstrong's development of the FM radio. Radios had become extremely popular in the 1920s. Radio transmitters sent out signals by systematically altering or "modulating" the height, or "amplitude," of the radio waves. Irritating static, however, was frequently a problem with amplitude-modulating (AM) radios. Electrical storms and nearby appliances in operation interfered with a radio transmitter's ability to modulate the complete radio transmission.

In 1939, Armstrong skirted this problem by devising a way to transmit radio signals by modulating the length, or "frequency," of the radio waves. His FM system could not tune in to stations more than a few miles away, but at close range it could provide static-free listening. Armstrong's invention upset powerful AM radio interests, and he had to battle them for twenty years before FM radio took root in the United States.

4

MEASUREMENT AND DETECTION

As early as 1849, scientists discovered how to use light reflection as a means of measurement. By sending a beam of light to a spot a known distance away and recording how long it took the reflection to return, they could calculate the speed of light. In 1917, scientists learned how to measure the speed of reflected sound to gain information about sea- and lake beds. Some wondered if they could use reflected light in the same way to locate objects in the sky.

MEASURING WITH RADIO WAVES

This proved to be impractical because light is so easily scattered, absorbed, or stopped by such things as fog and dust. Radio waves, on the other hand, are more easily focused and far more penetrating. The longer radio waves used in communication would be of no use for locating objects because they bend around objects instead of reflecting off them. But Scottish physicist Robert Watson-Watt discovered in the 1930s that very short radio waves, called microwaves, could penetrate fog yet reflect off moderate-sized objects.

Watson-Watt saw that microwaves could be used to track airplanes in flight. By 1935, he had designed and built a system that could send out microwaves and detect their reflected beam from aircraft at a distance of 40 miles (64 kilometers). His first transmitters could detect the presence of an aircraft but could not determine its direction or speed. This defect was quickly remedied with the use of transmitters that sent signals at regular intervals rather than in a continuous wave. The operator could determine the direction and speed of an object by the changes in time between the echoes.

The British government originally approached Watson-Watt to ask if he could possibly construct some kind of death ray. Watson-Watt instead proposed the more realistic military technology of radar.

The system eventually became known as radio detecting and ranging, which was shortened to *radar*.

In 1937, the British constructed a chain of twenty radar stations on their southern coast. The system improved with J. T. Randall and H. A. Boot's invention of the cavity magnetron, a practical, high-powered microwave generator whose pulses could be picked up by small receivers. This made portable radar possible. The British also developed a system for distinguishing friendly craft from enemy craft.

Radar's timely invention may well have saved Great Britain from destruction. In 1940, a superior German air force attempted to batter the British into surrendering. Radar technology warned the British well in advance of German air attacks. By giving a clear picture of the strength of the approaching German squadron, it allowed the outnumbered British air force to send its fighters where they were most needed. Unable to win control of the skies over Great Britain, the Germans eventually called off their invasion plans.

Microwave technology also proved to be of great use in tracking storms. A slightly different adaptation of microwaves has more recently been used in microwave ovens.

REVEALING THE SECRETS OF THE MICROSCOPIC WORLD

Waves of another nature led to the development of an instrument that could go far beyond the microscope in revealing the secrets of a world that was previously invisible to the human eye. Conventional optical microscopes were limited in their usefulness by the length of light waves. If an object was smaller than a light wave, that object could not be made visible with such a microscope.

By the 1930s, physicists had determined that electron waves were much shorter than light waves. German electrical engineer Ernst Ruska, along with Max Knoll, discovered a way to focus electron waves by means of a magnetic

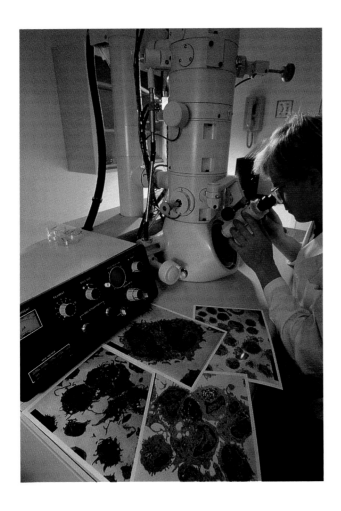

Modern electron microscopes developed from machines that were designed in the 1930s.

field. In 1931, Ruska built an electron microscope based on this technique. His microscope could magnify objects only 400 times, as opposed to about 2,000 times for a powerful light microscope. Several more years of tinkering were required for an electron microscope to match the capability of optical microscopes.

In 1937, Canadian physicist James Hillier, working without any outside funding, constructed a practical electron microscope that went far beyond optical microscopes in revealing the sights of the previously unseen world. His invention, which could magnify objects 7,000 times, quickly became a standard tool of microbiologists. Today, electron microscopes can magnify objects to more than two million times their normal size. This invention has allowed scientists to explore the structure of viruses and even large molecules.

In 1938, Australian-born American physicist Isidor Isaac Rabi discovered a complex measuring technique—magnetic resonance imaging (MRI). He

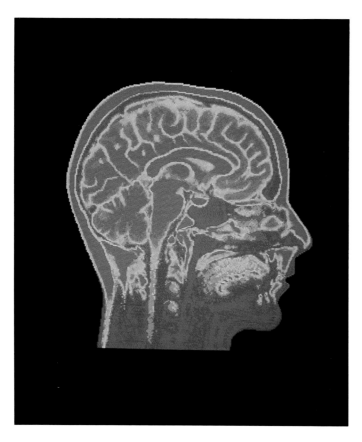

This false-color MRI scan shows the structure of the brain, spine, and facial tissues. Commonly used today, the magnetic resonance imaging technique was discovered in 1938.

found that he could excite protons by applying a strong magnetic field. The protons would send off faint radio signals. Rabi found that he could measure the amount of energy absorbed and given off by this process with great accuracy. In recent years, medical technicians have developed MRI machines that use this technique to reveal varying density of tissues. These are especially useful in diagnosing internal injuries such as brain damage.

5

CONSTRUCTION

Engineers and scientists sought to test the limits of their abilities in construction in the 1930s. Despite the fact that the world was mired in a cruel economic depression, they dreamed daring dreams. They took on massive, mind-boggling, seemingly impossible projects and created breathtaking structures that made observers wonder if there were any problems that human brains could not solve.

BRIDGING THE GAP

The 1930s was a decade of breakthroughs in bridges. Bridges are one of the underrated achievements of technology. They make travel so easy between towns, cities, and states that people take them for granted. Yet a single bridge closed for construction in a small city can create terrible traffic jams and countless headaches. In the 1930s, engineers reached out to provide comfortable travel between points that few people thought could ever be connected by concrete and steel.

When the Brooklyn Bridge opened in 1883, awed observers called it one of the wonders of the world. But in 1931, a new structure opened in New York City that easily claimed the title of the world's most spectacular bridge. Spanning the Hudson River, the George Washington Bridge was 3,500 feet (1,067 meters) long, more than twice as long as the Brooklyn Bridge.

On January 5, 1933, an even more majestic bridge began to take shape on the opposite coast of the United States. For many years, citizens in the San Francisco peninsula area had speculated on the possibility of bridging the ocean channel that cut the city off from towns and cities to the north. Most conceded that it was impossible. Any bridge would have to be built across nearly a mile of open sea buffeted by ocean tides and high winds.

Men, women, and children strolled across the Golden Gate Bridge on its opening day.

The Golden Gate Bridge still attracts visitors to San Francisco.

But bridge builder Joseph Strauss argued, "Our world of today revolves completely around things which at one time couldn't be done because they were supposedly beyond the limits of human endeavor." He spent twelve years convincing people that he could accomplish the feat.

Everything about the Golden Gate Bridge, as the structure was called, defied belief. The longest section of the bridge alone spanned 4,200 feet (1,280 meters) of ocean. The Golden Gate Bridge was such an ambitious undertaking that twenty-seven years would pass before a longer span was built. Each of the cables that supported the bridge weighed more than a heavy cruiser. Each of the end towers of the bridge was taller than the Washington Monument and was constructed of more than 44,000 tons (39,600 metric tons) of steel.

The Golden Gate Bridge eliminated one of the major traffic headaches in the world at the time. Before the bridge was opened on May 28, 1937, traffic from San Francisco either had to take a long circuit around to the south or take a ferry across the bay. On holiday weekends, the line of cars waiting for ferries could stretch as far as 10 miles (16 kilometers).

TOUCHING THE SKY

Another technological challenge tackled by engineers in the 1930s was the construction of structures that rose so high in the air they were nicknamed skyscrapers. The greatest of these was the Empire State Building in New York City. Built on a steel cage frame that can rock 1.5 inches (3.8 centimeters) either way in the wind, the 102-story Empire State Building stood 1,250 feet (381 meters) high, dwarfing all other buildings in existence.

The Empire State Building was constructed as an office building but was viewed as more of a curiosity in its early years than as a functioning property. Because of a lack of tenants, it was known for years among locals as the Empty State Building.

HOLDING BACK THE RIVER

Engineers took on a different sort of monster project in the arid American Southwest when they sought to dam the Colorado River. The dam, originally called the Boulder Dam and later known as the Hoover Dam, required as much concrete as a paved highway stretching from San Francisco to New York. The pressure of such a mass of concrete would create so much heat that engineers estimated it would take a century for the dam to cool and harden.

Project designers eliminated this problem by installing miles of 1-inch (2.5-centimeter) pipe in the concrete as it was poured. They then brought in a gigantic cooling system capable of freezing 1,000 tons (900 metric tons) of ice per day. This pumped cold water through the pipes, which took away the heat and allowed the concrete to harden within a few months.

The Hoover Dam, completed in 1936, was an impressive technological achievement.

The Boulder Dam, finished in 1936, created Lake Mead, the world's largest reservoir, and provided electrical power for 1.5 million customers.

WORKING WITH NEW MATERIALS

Scientists in the 1930s helped engineers in their quest to build new structures and products by developing new materials. Both plastics and metal alloys provided strength and durability that had previously been unavailable to builders. Another new material became available, more or less by accident, as the glass industry looked for new uses for its product. Glass had many advantages over other materials—it did not burn, rot, or rust. It would not melt except under extremely hot temperatures. It was waterproof, resisted acids, and could be stretched into various shapes. The main problem that

A Corvette with a body of reinforced fiberglass went on sale in the 1930s.

limited its use was that it broke so easily. Because glass was so fragile, many industries in the 1930s were replacing it with new plastic materials, which had similar advantages to glass but were more durable.

The Owens-Illinois Glass Company hired a consultant named Games Slayter to help find new products for glass. While Slayter was touring an Owens-Illinois Glass Company factory in Ohio, he noticed a pile of melted glass by a furnace opening. The air pressure of the hot furnace had blown the glass into long, thin fibers. Normally, this glass was thrown away. But Slayter took a closer look at the material. In this form, glass was not fragile. It had all the advantages of glass without that one glaring defect.

Soon the company began putting out a new line of products that made use of this material, which was known as fiberglass. This material has proven useful in air filters, insulation, fishing poles, boat and automobile bodies, tanks, pipes, and many other products.

6

OUTER SPACE

In the mid-nineteenth century, astronomers noticed that the planet Uranus veered slightly off of its expected orbit. Several of them suggested that this could be caused by the gravitational pull of some large object in the vicinity—perhaps a planet. They made careful calculations to determine the most likely location of such a heavenly body. Sure enough, in 1846 astronomers discovered Neptune in almost precisely the spot that had been predicted.

THE SEARCH FOR PLANET X

Further calculations, however, showed that Neptune's gravity could not completely account for Uranus's peculiar orbit. Astronomer Percival Lowell believed that an even more distant unknown planet, which he called Planet X, was exerting a gravitational pull. He became almost obsessed with calculating where this planet should be and trying to locate it through a telescope. Lowell spent the last eleven years of his life searching for Planet X. He never did find what he was looking for. His friends believed that his failure to find the planet virtually killed him.

But following Lowell's death, astronomers at Lowell's observatory in Arizona continued the search. The task of sifting through the millions of stars in the skies for a tiny pinprick of a planet was overwhelming. In 1929, astronomers at the Lowell Observatory hired a young assistant to handle the work. They selected Clyde Tombaugh, a twenty-two-year-old Kansas farmboy. Although he had no education beyond high school, Tombaugh had spent his winters building his own telescopes and viewing the sky.

Tombaugh carried out his assignment by photographing small sections of the sky and then photographing the same sections a day or two later. He then compared the first photograph with the second to see if any of the

Clyde Tombaugh, the discoverer of the planet Pluto

"stars" had moved. Planets revolve around the sun, while stars remain stationary. Therefore, if any dot had moved, that would indicate it was a planet and not a star.

The process of examining the photographs, some of which contained as many as 400,000 stars, was tedious and time-consuming. On thousands of occasions, what looked like a possible planet turned out to be nothing more than a flaw in the film. Tombaugh later noted that prominent astronomers "told me that I was wasting my time."

On January 23, 1930, Tombaugh photographed a section of the sky in the constellation Gemini. Six days later, he again photographed the section. While comparing the two photographs on February 18, he noticed that one tiny dot in the first picture had moved just slightly in the second. This moving object had to be a planet. Tombaugh determined that it was beyond Neptune, very near the spot where Lowell had predicted Planet X should be.

On March 13, 1930, the seventy-fifth anniversary of Percival Lowell's birth, the Lowell Observatory astronomers announced the discovery of this planet. They named it Pluto, after the Greek god of the underworld, primarily because the first two letters were the same as Percival Lowell's initials. Pluto had actually been photographed more than a dozen times before Tombaugh's discovery. Lowell himself had captured it on film without realizing it was a planet. On one occasion when it might have been discovered, Pluto's image had fallen exactly on a flaw in the film and so had escaped detection.

Ironically, Pluto turned out to be an incredible fluke. Astronomers determined that it was a very small planet, about two-thirds the diameter of the earth's moon, with about one-fifth of the moon's mass. Such a small planet could not possibly have exerted the gravitational pull on Uranus that astronomers had observed. In other words, even though Tombaugh found Pluto very near the spot where Lowell had directed him, it could not have been the Planet X that Lowell had predicted.

Pluto remains a puzzlement to astronomers today. Its size and its extremely irregular orbit (part of its orbit brings it much closer than Neptune to the sun) leave doubt as to what kind of body Pluto is.

IN THE RIGHT PLACE AT THE RIGHT TIME

Another accidental discovery occurred when the Bell Telephone Laboratories assigned one of its employees, Karl Jansky, to work on the problem of radio static. While probing into the sources of the irritating static that interrupted radio broadcasts, Jansky heard a weak static of a kind he had not heard before. It was not coming from the earth but from overhead.

At first he thought the interference was coming from the sun. But the hissing sound became stronger each time his rotating antenna focused on the constellation Sagittarius.

Jansky's discovery of radio signals coming from far off in the galaxy caused an immediate sensation. One radio host broadcast the sounds Jansky was hearing with the announcement, "I want you to hear for yourself this radio hiss from the depths of the universe."

But after the initial excitement, there did not seem to be much that could be done with the information. Jansky went on to other projects and the subject of radio waves from beyond the earth went nowhere for a number of years.

It was revived in 1937 by American radio engineer Grote Reber. Purely out of personal curiosity about the radio waves that Jansky had discovered, Reber built a large disk, 31 feet (9.5 meters) in diameter, in his backyard so that he could study radio waves from outer space. Reber's neighbors had no idea as to the purpose of the strange contraption. Some thought it was for collecting water; others guessed it was an attempt to control the weather. The device, known as a radio telescope, could reflect and focus these waves so that Reber could measure their intensity.

Reber found that the intensity of radio waves varied. Some points, particularly the center of the Milky Way and certain constellations, emitted

Today's radio telescopes are based on a strange device built by Grote Reber in 1937.

much more intense radio waves than the general background from outer space. Reber was the world's first radio astronomer. Eventually, radio telescopes became an important tool in helping astronomers gain information about the universe. Currently radio astronomers are listening to radio waves to try and determine if intelligent life exists elsewhere in the universe.

INCREDIBLE BLACK HOLES

Not all of the advances in astronomy in the 1930s came about by accident. One of the most mind-stretching discoveries in history resulted from a complex series of mathematical calculations.

Astronomers Fritz Zwicky and Walter Baade and a young Indian student named Subrahmanyan Chandrasekhar used their knowledge of gravity, astronomy, and nuclear physics to develop a theory of neutron stars. They proposed that when stars begin to use up the nuclear fuel that causes them to burn, they begin to cool. As they do so, the effect of gravity becomes stronger and the outer parts of the star are pulled in toward the center.

Chandrasekhar noted that in medium-sized stars, the force of gravity could compress the star until it was a "white dwarf," a tiny star about 10,000 times as dense as the earth. Zwicky and Baade calculated that in larger stars,

Chandrasekhar presented a paper, in which he discussed the subject of ultradense stars collapsed down to almost no volume, at a prestigious meeting of astronomers. Expecting to receive recognition for his findings, he was stunned when Sir Arthur Eddington, the world's foremost astronomer at the time, stood up and ridiculed Chandrasekhar's ideas.

the pressure would be so great that it would crush electrons into the nucleus, where they would combine with the protons to form neutrons. This would create a neutron star—a superdense star only a few miles in diameter, yet still maintaining its original mass.

The idea of atoms collapsing into material so dense that a thumbnail-sized piece would weigh more than a battleship was incredible enough. But astrophysicists playing around with the numbers and equations discovered an even more bizarre possibility. Chandrasekhar calculated that massive stars could have a gravitational force so strong that nothing could stop it. The star would keep collapsing until it took up virtually no volume yet retained its tremendous weight.

Subrahmanyan Chandrasekhar was awarded the Nobel Prize in physics in 1983 for his pioneering studies of the structure and evolution of stars.

The implications of this were stunning. People were being asked to imagine something that took up no space being so heavy that not even light could escape. Many scientists dismissed the notion as a fantasy. But in 1939, Robert Oppenheimer supported the new concept with mathematical calculations showing that a very large star would collapse to a point and create what came to be called a black hole.

Incredible as these ideas seemed at the time, convincing evidence of the existence of white dwarfs, neutron stars, and even black holes have come to pass.

PHOTOGRAPHING THE HEAVENS

The 1930s was also the decade in which astronomers pulled back the curtain on the universe. Prior to 1930, astronomers could photograph only a tiny portion of the sky at one time. But that year, an Estonian optician named Bernhard Schmidt arranged lenses and mirrors to create a new type of photographic telescope. Schmidt's wide-angle lens telescope has become an important tool for astronomers, enabling them to study much greater portions of the sky at once.

7

MEDICINE

Once scientists in the late nineteenth century had discovered the surprising truth that tiny organisms called bacteria and protozoans could cause deadly human diseases, medical researchers set out to find ways to destroy these menacing creatures without harming people.

LOOKING FOR A MAGIC BULLET

In 1907, German scientist Paul Ehrlich found a chemical that would attack bacteria responsible for syphilis yet was safe for humans. His arsenic compound, called salvarsan, set off a wide-scale search for similar chemicals and triggered hope that many diseases could soon be wiped out.

That did not happen. Salvarsan proved to be less than a miracle cure. It had dangerous side effects and required months, even years of painful injections. Meanwhile, the search for other effective chemicals turned up nothing. By 1930, according to medical experts, "The notion that new [disease-fighting] drugs might be discovered was a pipe dream."

The failure was particularly frustrating because scientists found many materials that would destroy harmful microbes in test tubes. But these products either showed no disease-fighting effect when given to live mice or were nearly as lethal to the mice as to the microbes.

Medical researchers did not give up, however. Some of them focused their attention on dyes. Many of these dyes were known to have the ability to combine with some cells and not with others. That led to the hope that perhaps they could interact with germ cells but not human cells.

Gerhard Domagk, research director for the huge German chemical manufacturing firm I. G. Farbenindustrie, ran tests on some of the company's dyes to see if any might have medical value. His thoroughness paid off during experiments with an orange red dye made from sulfanilamide. The compound, marketed under the name Prontosil Rubrum, barely disturbed bacteria in a test tube. Logically, Domagk could have concluded that there was no sense in further tests with the dye. But Domagk continued experimenting with the compound. When he injected it into diseased mice, it proved remarkably effective. In 1932, he injected twenty-six test animals with lethal hemolytic streptococci bacteria. Twelve of these animals received a single dose of Prontosil. Each of them survived. Meanwhile, all fourteen of the animals that received no treatment died within four days. Further tests showed that the dye appeared to have no harmful side effects for the mice.

Domagk took great care to guarantee that his findings were accurate before he reported them to the public. When he finally broke the news in 1935, doctors were surprised and delighted. They immediately began to use Prontosil to treat strep, spinal meningitis, pneumonia, and gonorrhea.

Domagk threw his usual caution to the wind when his young stepdaughter, Hildegaard, fell seriously ill from an infection after pricking her finger on a needle. After all other medical remedies failed, Domagk turned to his new drug, as yet untested on humans. He injected Hildegaard with a large dose of Prontosil and anxiously awaited the result. The young girl showed dramatic improvement and recovered completely.

A year later, Italian researcher Daniele Bovet solved the mystery of why Prontosil worked so well in live creatures but not in a test tube. When he reduced the complex compound to simpler components, he discovered that only part of the compound, sulfanilamide, had disease-fighting qualities. Bovet suggested that the dye as a whole was not effective against bacteria and so accomplished little in a test tube. But when injected into living creatures, it was broken down into its basic components. In this form, sulfanilamide could stop bacterial growth by depriving bacteria of nutrients.

The spectacular success of sulfanilamide led researchers to experiment with similar compounds. Many of these "sulfa drugs" proved to have wonderful bacteria-destroying powers yet remained harmless to humans. By 1942, more than 3,600 such compounds had been isolated. Many of them were used in treatment and saved thousands of lives.

A Second Look at a Bacteria Killer

The news that there really were compounds that could destroy bacteria without harming the host revived some research efforts that had lain dormant for a number of years. Since the 1870s, scientists had known that some microbes manufactured chemical substances that attacked other microbes. But this had not seemed of much value given the prevailing notion that what was harmful to bacteria was also harmful to humans. In fact, when Alexander Fleming of Scotland discovered the bacteria-killing power of a substance called penicillin produced by penicillium mold in 1928, no one paid much attention.

With the breakthrough in sulfa drugs, medical researchers began to take a second look at natural antibiotics. British scientists Howard Florey and Ernst Chain dug up Fleming's old paper on penicillin. They selected penicillin as one of three antibiotic agents they would use in tests. Unlike Fleming, who knew little about chemistry, Florey and Chain succeeded in isolating the antibiotic portion of penicillin from the mold in 1939.

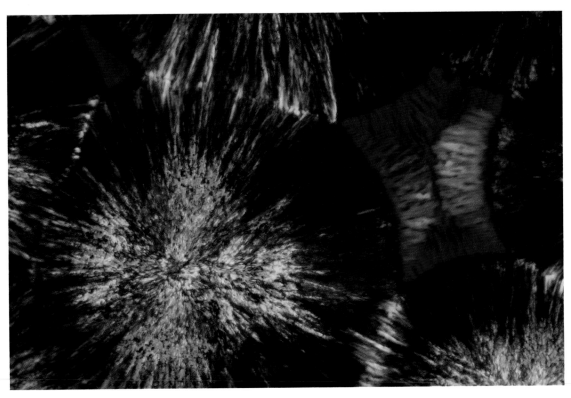

A false-color photomicrograph—picture taken through a microscope—of penicillin

The brown powder that they purified proved to be devastating to bacteria. Scientists could dilute the material a half million times and it still would kill disease-causing bacteria. Like sulfa drugs, penicillin directed all of its attack against bacteria and left the host alone. Within a decade, factories were pumping out penicillin in huge quantities. Many types of infections that had killed humans for centuries could suddenly be cured quickly and painlessly.

The discoveries of sulfa drugs and penicillin ushered medicine into a new era. Instead of helplessly standing by or merely trying to make sick patients as comfortable as possible, physicians now possessed extraordinary powers of healing. The use of drugs in fighting illness, pioneered during the 1930s, has skyrocketed ever since. As one medical expert put it, the medical discoveries of the 1930s have made scientists "obsessed with the idea of curing disease through medical research."

The Fight Against Viruses

A different sort of unseen enemy of the human body proved a more elusive foe than bacteria. The existence of viruses, living things too tiny to be seen with a microscope, had been demonstrated by the use of filters in 1898. Between that time and 1930, more than forty diseases, including measles, influenza, smallpox, and the common cold, had been linked to viruses. But scientists were totally baffled as to the nature of these destructive beings.

In 1931, English bacteriologist William Elford figured out a way to measure the size of viruses. He set up a system of filters, each filter having a more closely meshed membrane than the previous one so that it could block out ever smaller particles. Elford ran liquid that contained various viruses through this system. He proved that viruses could be sorted out and their sizes determined by the size of the mesh that prevented the viruses from passing. Elford's experiment showed that viruses were smaller than the smallest bacteria and that they came in a variety of sizes.

Scientists who attempted to study viruses were thwarted by the fact that viruses grow only in living cells. No laboratory could afford the many thousands of small animals needed to conduct experiments with viruses. American scientist Ernest Goodpasture solved the problem. While studying an agricultural disease called fowl pox, he observed that fertile chick eggs

Before the 1930s, only two virus vaccines existed: the smallpox vaccine developed by Edward Jenner and the rabies vaccine developed by Louis Pasteur. Both required living animals—cows in the case of smallpox and rabbits in the case of rabies—to culture the virus in the vaccine.

were an ideal environment for growing viruses. They were plentiful and inexpensive. Yet they provided a sterile environment—free from contamination with bacteria—and the living cells that the viruses needed to multiply.

Goodpasture's discovery cleared the way for virologists to grow the quantities of viruses they needed for their studies and for the production of vaccines against viral diseases. It was largely responsible for the development of an effective and affordable vaccine against polio, which crippled thousands of young people throughout the world in the first half of the twentieth century.

THE DREADED YELLOW FEVER

Yellow fever was one of the deadliest diseases known to humans in the 1930s. Near the turn of the century, American military surgeon Walter Reed had determined that mosquitoes transmitted the deadly disease. Prior to 1930, efforts at preventing the disease centered on reducing the mosquito population in areas where yellow fever commonly occurred. During that decade, scientists determined that viruses were the culprits in that disease. Attempts to develop a yellow fever vaccine seemed doomed by evidence that this virus was extremely difficult to study; it seemed to attack only humans and monkeys. Since researchers could not afford truckloads of monkeys for experimentation, development of a vaccine seemed doubtful.

Fortunately, a South African-born American named Max Theiler discovered that he could infect mice with the yellow fever virus if he injected pieces of infected monkey liver directly into their brains. He then found that as he passed the virus from one mouse to another, it gradually lost its lethal nature. After 176 passages from mouse to mouse, the virus no longer had any harmful effect on mice. Theiler used this tamed form of yellow fever virus as a vaccine, which was manufactured in large quantities using chick embryos. When the vaccine was injected into a human, the person's immune system built up a defense against it. This defense would then protect the person should a similar-appearing lethal yellow fever virus find its way into his or her system.

Theiler's vaccine saved the lives of thousands of American soldiers during World War II. Despite the fact that many American troops were stationed in areas where yellow fever was rampant, none died of the deadly disease during the war.

American researcher Wendell Stanley probably did as much as anyone to improve our knowledge of viruses. Prior to his work in the mid-1930s, no one had a clue as to what a virus was. Stanley obtained a large quantity of tobacco mosaic virus by mashing up a ton of infected tobacco leaves. He then ran a protein-extraction experiment, on the chance that viruses might prove to be made of proteins.

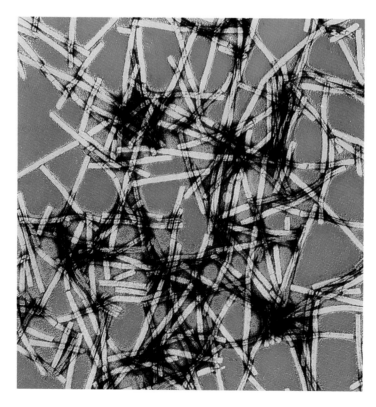

Wendell Stanley's work involved various experiments using the tobacco mosaic virus.

Sure enough, Stanley isolated a protein from his mixture, which he injected into healthy leaves. The protein turned out to be highly infectious. This proved that viruses were largely made up of proteins. Later he was able to prove that viruses were also composed of a small amount of nucleic acid. Stanley's discoveries provided direction for virologists probing the nature of viruses.

YOU ARE WHAT YOU EAT

Scientists also made the world a more healthy place in the 1930s with their work on nutrition. The importance of vitamins in maintaining health had been firmly established for two decades. Nevertheless, the kinds of foods that provided large amounts of these essential substances were not always readily available. Historians estimate that during World War I, half the Russian army suffered from a disease called scurvy, caused by a lack of vitamin C.

Efforts to study vitamin C progressed slowly because of the difficulty of finding significant concentrations of the vitamin in one place. Hungarian-born American researcher Albert Szent-Györgyi solved that problem when he discovered that red peppers contained an abundance of the material. (In the early days of his research, Szent-Györgyi had to grind up tons of animal adrenal glands to produce less than an ounce of vitamin C.)

Now able to obtain a reasonable quantity of the vitamin, researchers such as Szent-Györgyi and American chemist Charles King figured out its molecular structure in 1932. Using this information, Polish-born Swiss chemist Tadeus Reichstein created a synthetic form of vitamin C the following year. Manufacturers began

Albert Szent-Györgyi's research focused on vitamin C.

to crank out huge quantities of this essential ingredient and marketed the first vitamin pills.

Even Better Than Before

Later in the decade, researchers discovered that tiny amounts of certain minerals such as zinc were also crucial in keeping the body healthy. Food manufacturers began to fortify foods not only with vitamins but with these trace nutrients. For the first time in history, people could easily obtain all the essential vitamins and minerals they needed even if the proper foods were not readily available.

8

PHYSICS

In the 1930s, physicists became fascinated with the basic building blocks of the universe—atoms. In recent years, they had discovered that atoms consisted of a positively charged core of protons surrounded by a shell of negatively charged electrons. Furthermore, they had become aware of the tremendous energy locked up in the nucleus of the atom. According to calculations made by Albert Einstein, the conversion of a tiny amount of nuclear matter into energy would unleash an almost unimaginable burst of energy.

CHANGING THE NUCLEUS

In 1919, British physicist Ernest Rutherford showed that if high-energy particles struck a nucleus, they could knock loose a subatomic particle. Physicists became intrigued with the notion of altering the nuclei of atoms. What sort of changes could one produce in certain elements by tinkering with these elementary units of nature?

Unfortunately, bombarding a nucleus was not easy. Rutherford had managed a very limited bombardment using high-energy particles from radium, but this was a rare material. In their search for a particle to use as a bullet against atomic nuclei, scientists were thwarted by two facts: negatively charged electrons were too small to make an impact on a nucleus; and positively charged particles, although large enough, were repelled by the nucleus, which is also positively charged. The problem with these positive particles was how to get them moving at a high enough rate of speed that they could overcome the magnetic force of the nucleus.

Furthermore, Rutherford's radium particles did not strike the targeted nuclei often enough to provide scientists with measurable results. The nucleus of an atom was so tiny, like a dot in the center of a huge bubble, that it was extremely difficult to hit.

One of those who puzzled over these problems was Ernest Lawrence, a young man from Canton, South Dakota. Working at the University of California at Berkeley, Lawrence searched for ways to fire particles at atoms.

Physicists had already developed accelerators that could cause particles to move faster. But these accelerators had to be extremely long in order to build up the kind of speeds Lawrence was interested in. In the spring of 1929, Lawrence happened across an article describing an experiment by Norwegian Rolf Wideroe using positive ions (atoms that have lost their electrons and are positively charged). The article noted that when the ions were hit twice by a certain voltage, they traveled at twice the energy level of the voltage source.

Lawrence scribbled some quick calculations and decided that a voltage source should be able to increase the energy level (and therefore the velocity) of a particle each time it was applied. He then realized that if he constructed a circular track that kept steering the particles past the same voltage source time after time, he should be able to accelerate the particles to a tremendous speed.

Working on a tight budget, Lawrence had to use coffee cans, plate glass, copper, brass, sealing wax, and scraps of equipment to construct his device. In September of 1930, he succeeded in putting together a pie-shaped instrument that demonstrated his theory. A 4-inch (10-centimeter) brass chamber was connected to arms mounted between the poles of an electromagnet. The magnetic field was arranged to bend the path of the protons that were traveling through the chamber. At slower speeds, the magnets kept deflecting the protons back into the chamber, where they received successive charges that built up their energy. As these particles reached greater speeds, the magnets had less effect on them. Their path was altered from a circle to a spiral until the particles finally shot out an opening in the device at tremendous speed. Lawrence called his device a magnetic resonance accelerator. His assistants

Lawrence had once debated giving up his career as a physicist because he was afraid he was not smart enough to do the job.

Ernest Lawrence, the inventor of the cyclotron, and his first successful cyclotron, which he could hold in the palm of his hand.

referred to it as a cyclotron just to tease Lawrence, but that was the name that caught on.

In 1931, Lawrence built an 80,000-volt cyclotron. But he realized he needed an even more powerful device before he could start cracking open atomic nuclei. Using an 85-ton (77-metric-ton) magnet he found rusting in a dump, Lawrence built an accelerator capable of splitting open atoms in 1932.

Actually, a British team using a straight-line accelerator split off a particle from a small nucleus earlier that year. But Lawrence's cyclotron opened the way to large-scale experimentation with the entire spectrum of elements. Physicists have said that the cyclotron has revealed as many secrets in its time as the microscope. It allowed scientists to chart the nature of all the elements and eventually proved useful in medical research. Most importantly, it uncovered terrifying secrets about the universe that not even the most imaginative scientists could have predicted.

SECRETS OF THE NUCLEUS

One of the first secrets that particle accelerators helped discover was that the nucleus was not what scientists thought it was. For twenty years, physicists had assumed that an atomic nucleus was made up of protons and electrons. Nitrogen, for example, was found to have an atomic mass of 14, therefore its nucleus must be made of 14 protons. But nitrogen nuclei had an electrical charge of only 7. This could be explained by assuming that the nucleus also contained 7 negatively charged electrons. Although they were too small to significantly affect the atomic weight, the electrons would neutralize the charge of 7 of the protons. That meant a nitrogen nucleus had 21 particles: 14 protons and 7 electrons.

In 1925, however, scientists had concluded from measurements of particle spin that a nitrogen nucleus could not contain an odd number of particles. This puzzling finding led English physicist James Chadwick to believe that the nucleus might contain 7 protons and 7 proton-sized particles with a neutral charge. The problem in proving his theory was that scientists detected the presence of subatomic particles by means of their electrical charge. How could they detect a particle that had no charge?

Chadwick used a particle accelerator to help solve the problem. In 1932, he bombarded atoms of the element beryllium with alpha particles, which are the positively charged nuclei of the helium atom. He also placed some paraffin wax near the beryllium and observed what happened to it. Chadwick discovered that the paraffin was ejecting protons. The particles responsible for knocking these protons out of the paraffin had to have come from the beryllium.

Chadwick was unable to detect any charge in the particles escaping from the beryllium. Yet he knew that only a particle the size of a proton could blast protons out of the paraffin. Therefore, he could conclude that the nuclear particles leaving the beryllium were large neutral particles, which he called neutrons. Chadwick was able to measure the mass of a neutron, which he found to be slightly greater than the combined mass of a proton and an electron. Chadwick's discovery gave scientists new insight into the structure of atoms.

In 1934, the French husband and wife team of Frédéric and Irène Joliot-Curie used an accelerator to bombard aluminum atoms with alpha particles, which had now been determined to consist of 2 protons and 2 neutrons. The Joliot-Curies observed that some of the aluminum nuclei absorbed one of these high-energy alpha particles and ejected a neutron. Aluminum had been found to consist of 13 protons and 14 neutrons, adding up to an atomic number of 27. By ingesting an alpha particle (2 protons and 2 neutrons) and releasing a proton, the nucleus now contained 14 protons and 16 neutrons for an atomic number of 30. This happened to be the atomic number for an entirely different element, silicon-30. In other words, their bombardment had changed aluminum atoms into silicon-30 atoms.

More astounding yet, the Joliot-Curies discovered that in some cases the bombarded aluminum nucleus ejected a neutron instead of a proton. That resulted in nuclei with 15 protons and 15 neutrons, to make up the element phosphorus-30. When the scientists stopped their bombardment, they found that the radiation, or ejection of particles, continued. The phosphorus-30 was radioactive, that is, it had been put into such an excited, unstable state that it kept kicking out protons until it reached the stable configuration of the silicon-30.

The Joliot-Curies had created the world's first artificial radioactivity from an ordinary stable element. Lawrence's increasingly powerful cyclotrons gave scientists the means to bombard one element after another, to create radioactive forms of the element or even to create new elements altogether.

Among those joining the flurry of nuclear bombardment was Italian physicist Enrico Fermi. Fermi had deduced that Chadwick's discovery, the neutron, might be an even more suitable particle for experimentation than protons or alpha particles. Unlike positively charged particles, which are repelled by the positive force of the nucleus, neutrons would not be repelled at all. Therefore, they could enter a nucleus without having to be energized to fantastic speeds. Slow-moving neutrons were more likely to be absorbed by the nucleus rather than blast pieces off the nucleus.

Fermi found that, after firing neutrons at a target, he could slow the neutrons down by passing them through a moderator such as water or paraffin. He tried using slowed neutrons as his bullets in the bombardment of uranium.

Uranium has 92 protons, more than any other natural element. Fermi hoped that he could get the huge uranium nucleus to absorb a neutron. He expected this would lead to a chain of events that would cause the now unstable nucleus to emit a negative particle. This would convert one of the neutral particles into a proton and give him an entirely new element with 93 protons.

Fermi was initially convinced that he had created this new element in his experiments, but his results were confusing. In 1938, German physicist Otto Hahn set out to unravel what had gone on in Fermi's experiment. Hahn suspected that some uranium was being changed into other elements. When Hahn repeated Fermi's work and carefully examined the results of the uranium bombardment, he found not only traces of radioactive uranium but also a small amount of the metal barium.

Since there had been no barium in the original sample, the only explanation was that some of the uranium had changed into barium. But barium, with an atomic number of 56, was much lighter than uranium. Scientists agreed that all atomic nuclei remained basically intact throughout all types of particle bombardment. The only changes were the loss or gain of a particle or two, or the creation of instability, which caused the nuclei to disintegrate a few pieces at a time through radioactivity—the release of particles. But in order for uranium to change into barium, a uranium nucleus would have to be cut almost in half!

The notion that the enormous forces that held a nucleus together could fall apart simply by the introduction of neutrons was so absurd that Hahn dared not announce what he had learned for fear of being ridiculed. His report on his experiment did not mention this result.

But he privately explained his findings in a letter to his colleague of more than thirty years, Lise Meitner. Meitner was an Austrian Jew who had recently fled to Sweden to escape the Nazi persecutions.

Meitner's nephew, physicist Otto Frisch, happened to be with Meitner when the letter arrived. "I found her at breakfast brooding over a letter from Hahn," he reported later. Puzzled by Hahn's information, Meitner and Frisch went for a walk in the snow. The two wrestled with the strange evidence before them. How was it possible? they asked over and over. How could the immensely powerful attractive forces holding a nucleus together be broken by a single neutron?

Eventually, they concluded that the uranium nucleus was so fragile that

Lise Meitner was awarded a prize in 1955 for her achievements in nuclear research. Presenting the prize is her longtime friend and colleague, Otto Hahn.

a small bump from a neutron would be enough to split it apart. Meitner calculated the energy that must be released from this splitting, which Frisch labeled fission, and found that it was mind-boggling. More assertive than Hahn, Meitner announced the findings to the world in January of 1939.

Scientists were particularly fascinated by the tremendous amount of energy unleashed when an atom was split. Yet there did not seem to be any way to collect or harness this energy, the product of these minute explosions.

UNLEASHING A TERRIBLE ENERGY

In the spring of 1939, however, scientists discovered a by-product of uranium fission that sent chills down their spines. Three groups of physicists demonstrated that, during fission, some of the uranium atoms released several neutrons. This pointed squarely to the possibility of a chain reaction: One neutron could strike a uranium atom and split it. This caused the atom to release energy and kick out two neutrons. These neutrons could then each strike one of the surrounding uranium atoms. These atoms would split, releasing more energy and more neutrons. Before long, hundreds, thousands, then millions of neutrons would be flying around, splitting uranium atoms and releasing energy. Although each atom was too tiny to provide a noticeable amount of energy, the combined force of millions of atoms giving off this energy would be incredible.

This information puzzled scientists. If a single stray neutron could set off such a chain reaction in uranium, then what had stopped such a reaction from occurring in nature and blowing up the world?

A few years before the discovery of fission, Canadian-born physicist Arthur Dempster, working in the United States, found that two forms of uranium existed in nature. Most uranium had 92 protons and 146 neutrons for an atomic weight of 238. But a rare form of uranium, less than 1 percent, consisted of 92 protons and 143 neutrons, for an atomic weight of 235.

Dempster's finding did not seem important at the time. But in 1939, Niels Bohr seized upon it as the answer to why the world had not blown up. He calculated that only the U-235 form of uranium could sustain the chain reaction of fission. This form was too rare and dispersed in nature to sustain a reaction on its own. Further experiments by physicists in the United States confirmed that Bohr's hunch was correct.

Some physicists, however, immediately saw that if U-235 could be concentrated, it very likely could sustain a chain reaction that would unleash unimaginable energy. Their calculations showed that the fissioning of a gram of uranium could produce ten million times the energy produced in burning a gram of coal.

Hungarian-born Leo Szilard, another of the scientific exiles who had fled Europe for fear of Hitler, understood what this meant. Szilard had been considering the possibility of a nuclear chain reaction since 1932. He had believed it impossible because he did not believe that the neutrons ejected from uranium could travel fast enough to knock neutrons out of other atoms. But when he heard the results of fission experiments in 1939, he realized that

Adolf Hitler personally cost Germany its leading role in scientific research. His campaign of terror against Jews chased away many of Germany's top scientists. Hitler also steered money and research efforts away from other scientific pursuits and into his own pet projects. As a result of this drain on its scientific resources, Germany never was, despite Szilard's fears, a serious threat to produce an atomic bomb during World War II.

a chain reaction was possible. All that was needed was to purify and concentrate enough uranium-235 to get the reaction going.

Szilard saw the possibility that a lightning-fast chain reaction could be used to create a devastating atomic bomb. Fearful of what would happen to the world if Hitler possessed such a weapon, he persuaded the influential physicist Albert Einstein to alert the government of the United States. On August 2, 1939, Einstein wrote a letter to President Franklin Roosevelt in which he explained how "extremely powerful bombs of a new type" could be built using the principles of nuclear physics.

Prodded by this warning, the United States embarked on a massive project to develop an atomic bomb. By the middle of 1945, it had succeeded.

The world had entered a new age of terrifying possibilities. The great superpowers engaged in such a furious race to build up their military might that they stockpiled enough warheads to destroy the world many times over. Scientists sought to harness the incredible power of the atom for the benefit of humankind. But even the nuclear power plants that were constructed to provide energy for peaceful purposes raised serious protests, especially when people faced the problem of disposing of the toxic by-products of creating that power.

The unleashed power of the atom not only threatened the security of the earth, it also shook the foundations of science. Scientists, formerly regarded as marvelous magicians who were constantly improving the world in which we live, now took on a suspicious cast. People, even guilt-ridden scientists themselves, began to question the wisdom of uncontrolled scientific progress. Science, which had provided humans with their brightest hope for a better future, now provided people with their greatest dread.

While little if any of this debate crossed peoples' minds in the 1930s, virtually all of the groundwork for the atomic age was laid during that fateful decade.

Further Reading

Aaseng, Nathan. *Twentieth Century Inventors.* New York: Facts on File, 1991.

Asimov, Isaac. *How Did We Find Out About Computers?* New York: Walker and Co., 1984.

_____. *How Did We Find Out About Pluto?* New York: Walker and Co., 1991.

_____. *How Did We Find Out About Vitamins?* New York: Walker and Co., 1974.

Balcziak, B. *Television.* Vero Beach, Florida: Rourke, 1989.

Calabro, Marian. *Zap! A Brief History of Television.* New York: Macmillan, 1992.

Gottfried, Ted. *Enrico Fermi.* New York: Facts on File, 1992.

Helicopters. North Bellmore, N.Y.: Marshall Cavendish, 1990.

Hitzeroth, Deborah. *Radar: The Silent Detector.* San Diego: Lucent Books, 1990.

Kaye, Judith. *The Life of Alexander Fleming.* New York: Twenty-First Century Books, 1993.

Lampton, Christopher. *Rocketry: From Goddard to Space Travel.* New York: Franklin Watts, 1988.

Otfinoski, Steven. *Igor Sikorsky.* Vero Beach, Florida: Rourke, 1993.

Streissguth, Tom. *Rocket Man: The Story of Robert Goddard.* Minneapolis: Carolrhoda, 1995.

Tames, Richard. *Alexander Fleming.* New York: Franklin Watts, 1990.

Index

photocopying, 34, 35
Piccard, Auguste, 23, 24
planes, 27, 28
plastic, 13, 15, 38, 48, 49
Pluto, 52, 53
polio, 61
positive ions, 66
proton, 68-70
protozoans, 57

Rabi, Isidor Isaac, 43, 44
radar, 42
radio, 36, 38, 42, 44
radioactivity, 10, 69
radio telescope, 53-54, *54*
radio waves, 39, 41, 53, 54
radium, 65
Reber, Grote, 53, 54
Reed, Walter, 61
refrigerants, 16
refrigerators, 16, *16*, 17
rockets, 25-27
rocket propulsion, 27
Rutherford, Ernest, 10, 65

Sikorsky, Igor, 29, *30*, 30
silk, 11, 15
skyscrapers, 47
Slayter, Games, 49
static, 35, 39, 53
stratosphere, 11, 23
subatomic particles, 65, 68
sulfanilamide, 58
Szent-Györgyi, Albert, 63, *63*
Szilard, Leo, 72, 73

tape recorder, 38
technicolor, 38
Teflon, *14*, 15
television, 31, 36-38
tobacco mosaic virus, 62, *62*
Tombaugh, Clyde, 51-52, *52*, 53
Turing, Alan, 32
typhus, 10, 18

ultraviolet radiation, 24
uranium, 69-73
Uranus, 51, 53

vaccine, 61, 62
vacuum tubes, 31
viruses, 43, 60-63
vitamins, 63, 64
Von Braun, Wernher, 26, 27

Warsitz, Erich, 26-28
Watson-Watt, Robert, 41, 42
Whittle, Frank, 27, 28
wide-angle lens telescope, 56
Woodbury, Daniel, 31, 33
World War I, 9, 18, 63
World War II, 18, 27-30, 32, 38, 39, 62, 73
Wright brothers, 28

yellow fever, 18, 61, 62

Zworykin, Vladimir, 36, 37, *37*

About the Author

Nathan Aaseng attended Luther College in Iowa and earned a B.A. degree with majors in both English and biology. He was particularly interested in the communication of scientific information to general audiences. After working for four years as a research microbiologist, he turned to writing full time.

Mr. Aaseng has written more than 100 books, primarily nonfiction for younger readers. He currently lives in Eau Claire, Wisconsin, with his wife and four children.